The D&I Manual

Diversity and Inclusion – An experienced and experiential, research-based thesis.

Wellbeing by way of self and social awareness.

Shipra Tripathi

ISBN: 979-8-89067-082-3

DEDICATION

In sincere memory of my late grandparents, Shri. Rudra Pati Tripathi and Smt. Vidya Tripathi, for all the lineage and love that has become my existential being.

To my beloved parents, Mr. Narendra Kumar Tripathi, Mrs. Kanak Tripathi and my doting brother Mr. Harsh Tripathi, one can only dream of a family this kind and loving. A book on diversity and inclusion cannot do without sincere gratitude to one's own family, all I am is all of you.

All my near and dear ones have had a profound impact on me and one would find yourself in my words and essence in this book. You belong.

I humbly acknowledge that this is solely my work, based out of my experience and thought.

Literary references are given in the 'reference' section.

I dedicate this literary body of work to each individual who forms the society.

CONTENT

9

ACKNOWLEDGEMENT

The author has summarised personal views and stated that when or rather first by taking care of one's own peace of mind and material and social existence and accepting it for what it is/being content with it, only then can one/I happily communicate and share it with others.

Secondly, being peaceful with myself, enables me to be acceptable to their truth and create happier acceptance of their truth.

Hence, while the author has shared the acceptance memo creation for self, in parallel socially stated and accepted it and in being truly the stated self, has created acknowledgment mechanisms for the people deemed as community and society, and accepted their reality. This is the overarching third person view, desirable for social well-being.

All by way of mindfulness.

This narrative has been created to fulfil the overarching purpose to create a diverse and inclusive world that is rooted in well-being, peace and prosperity. By creating the whole document in third person narrative, the author creates acceptance and validation of the narrative by the whole as one community.

Hence the statement of being or adherence to the narrative by people besides the author, in their first person or personal narratives - in whatever merit people deem fit for their own purpose to accept and acknowledge the narrative.

INTRODUCTION

D&I is widely used in the corporate sector as an acronym to the syllable 'Diversity and Inclusion', at times also known as DE&I, Diversity, Equity & Inclusion.

While it's been a segment in corporate governance for smooth functionality of organisations, it's been largely talked and discussed as a wing of corporations that makes employees from walks of life feel more enabled at work. People who identify as minority or seem to lack equitable career advancements are voluntarily and consciously provided fair aids to equate them at work. People who identify differently from a majoritarian view, be it in mind or body, are provided parity by counselling, consultation, education, awareness. An environment of kindred fellowship in organisations and communities is enabled by this conduct to avail higher degree of functionality.

This book takes on an individualistic perspective on the thought. Deep diving and understanding the situation from one's own point of view, another's point of view and a social/community point of view. Thus enabling an individual to be wiser in one's own inclusivity and behavioural norms when in society.

Body of work detailed in this book conveys the impact of mindfulness as a mandatory practice for peaceful collaboration.

The learning by doing approach initiates an interactive approach towards self and people and develops a more observational and stoic point of view/perspective, to observe the scope of absorption of internal and external opinion by considering the situation in third person.

The objective of personal and social well-being through mindfulness is made viable by exercise and observation.

The book entails the thesis in a cohesive and comprehensive narrative.

ESSENCE

Cycle of life is directly linked to life cycle and much of it is linked to mindset.

This is not a theoretical concept, it's one of rationale and measure.

As be the concepts of 'adi-anant' in mythology, translated to 'without beginning and end, everlasting, beyond space and time', the human existence and capabilities to perceive life and oneself is without array. Since, all tangible constructs of time and space and materialism like hour, weight etc are man-made, a person's theological perception of self is not dependent on these factors.

Reminding the humans that the finite and infinite co-exists as measures of one entity, starting from a tiny particle of energy in the form of light as a photon to universal wholeness as one giant essence of energy. Substance is absolute.

The universe, the universal energy existing in different forms and life energy as a part, is absolute. It collates and depletes giving us multiple experiences of existential plethora.

That said and understood, we imbibe the rationale in our day-to-day life for mindfulness and co-habitance.

Inclusivity for self by way of mindfulness, which self governs and creates a peaceful measure of coexistence.

The universal cycle of life and life cycle is a direct replica of humanly created societies and organisations and is also a direct replication of how our human minds work, how singular or collective human life interacts with the surrounding world.

A person's mindset is the sole proprietor for all peace and war.

This book talks about acceptance and evolution in any given situation, being on the same lines as the saying 'change your mind, change your life' but by way of consistency.

Consistent social well-being by way of consistent mindfulness.

It is the formal guidebook to becoming self-sustaining universal energy which is absolute in essence.

Thus, when the smallest speck in the universal faculty of existence, the human being, self-regulates one's own mind, body and soul aka life energy, an absolute sense of peace can sustain oneself.

When one practises this for another and takes it beyond, one can sustain an absolutely functional self in the world.

When each one of us sustains a sense of social wellbeing, we have an absolutely diverse and inclusive world.

A world that is diverse and inclusive of one and all by one and all.

20

STATEMENT

The D&I Manual is a compilation of my journals on how to maintain a stoic perspective for people management and derive productivity sustainably for oneself and the community. It's a self validation guide book, shared in a literary format.

I was 18 when I decided to study outside of my hometown, I thought myself completely naive and theological and one who needed authentic learning-by-doing self and social awareness. By the age of 24, I had taken myself through a bachelor's degree in pharmacy and a full-time MBA.

Short to a decade, by the age of 32, I found myself having worked across sectors in the business and marketing wing of corporations, from a sincere intern in my early professional days to the head of function in the domain.

By my 32nd birthday, on 17th December 2021, I had an idea and a belief, of what to do next but it was nascent and in a seed stage. Irrespective of any other person's involvement, I was not prepared for how to go about it or what to do next. I studied some more for good. Created something of value. A thought model was done by March 2022. March 2022 to 2023 has been about collating a construct for implementing the thought.

The primary objective has been to ideate and give physical form to an actionable construct. A 'self and social' approach i.e person and people approach, be it for or by individual or organisation, to diversity and inclusion.

Answering the quest - how can one follow a step by step process of communication to create compassionate environments for healthy, peaceful and growth oriented functionality.

Statement of purpose - how can just about anybody understand diversity and inclusion protocols and make them happen.

Activity - Sustainable growth via understanding and implementation of the self and the environment.

Please note, while the book is inclusive and functional-for-all, written in a purpose-driven overarching third person narrative, I have retained some of my personal experiences/journals and expressions in this narrative, shared as 'Author's note'. One may wonder about the need for sharing a personal work-life timeline, this is because the book is a dedicated work of nearly two years, based on a life lived across the years. The practical adherence of the theory as stated could only be retained, vindicated and sustained by introducing the experienced and experiential acumen.

'The D&I Manual' is a strategic compilation. Strategic in the fact that self and social awareness are theoretical and intangible components unique to each person. Thus, ascertained facts found true by virtue of practical adherence have been shared as a practical guidebook to hone one's personal/business communication and inclusivity skills.

I hope the book makes for valuable reading to whosoever interacts with this body of work.

Shipra Tripathi

23

24

ABSTRACT

Technically the usability of the expression is self expression, which is to speak the truth, say which is true and be accepting in nature.

Thus, establishing a favourable ecosystem for oneself, by creating a warm heart and a calm mind that is appreciative of the self and others.

Contrary to popular theories that the highest form of self actualization is achieved when a person's basic and aspirational requirements are met, the diversity and inclusion manual entails a mind-first approach to the process of self and social actualization.

The book is a compilation of observations and experiences of real life wherein people do actually accept life as is, by simply accepting the situation for what it is. Hence, sustaining a calm mind.

Thus enabling the possibility and creation of a favourable approach to life, in mind, body, soul and society.

Part I of this work is to enable inclusivity for oneself - by statement of thought at each stage of being and fixture of facts pertaining to it, as per all spheres of life.

The occurrence of thought, acknowledgment and acceptance of the thought and bringing oneself to an understanding of self and hence being at peace with nothingness, leading the pathway to being at peace with nowness.

One needs to state everything, one fact at a time. This is a direct step to looking at one's own self from a second and eventually a third person's perspective.

Part II of the book is a statement of thought and self to oneself. Acknowledging that we are all different energy embodiments and seeing oneself as part of the all encompassing and ever-finite part of the universe. Creation, emergence and submergence from one and the same source, time and again.

Acceptance, stating, nullifying and being at peace with the void and also the self that exists in the void.

Put out, stated in a factual chronological order, enabling the whole process.

Part III of the work for creating inclusivity is social awareness by way of realism.

Stating actionable facts as concepts to cater to different arenas of life, one must realise how this knowledge can be converted into something useful for sustainable development.

Practice for the statement of the understanding of the higher level of self and social construct.

Part IV of the book decidedly intertwines how a person's life, which is the cycle of life, is directly linked to the universal life cycle.

This part of the book explains the role of mindfulness or contentment for sustainable action.

It's an approach to an actionable way of conscious living pertaining to inclusivity in diversity, enabling one to make peace at every stage of life or situational occurrence of diversity, by employing fact based social norms for equality and inclusivity.

Part V, details revitalising authenticity in the self and the situation by way of practice.

The objective of this thesis is to substantiate the thought that for creating an inclusive environment, it's imperative that we as individuals inculcate a neutral point of view.

Since each individual is unique, a person's psychological makeup may be aligned with either stage of narration in the book, from Part I to V, at the moment of interaction with the book.

Also, as we grow, live, the stages are intermittent, at each stage we need to know and perceive the situation appropriately and evolve as a calmer, more functional social being.

The actualization lies in the details and practice.

28

PREFACE

To create a medium and an environment for D&I with collaborative content, it's imperative that we as individuals inculcate a neutral point of view.

The objective of this thesis/body of work is to substantiate the value of mindfulness for overall well being for the self and community as a whole.

The model implements the thought that well-being and inclusivity can be implemented by self in one's own nativity and for creating an inclusive environment, by being enabled further in one's social capacity.

"Warm-heartedness leads to a healthy mind. Peace of mind allows us to sleep soundly. I'm not talking about the benefits of the next life or of finding God, but of being a peaceful person with a calm mind and a warm heart here and now.", Dalai Lama.

To do,

Step 1. Be - inculcate a neutral point of view.

Step 2. Belong - observe to learn better.

Step 3. Communicate - evolve to be better.

Step 4. Simplicity - sustain.

Step 5. Authenticity - revitalise.

STRUCTURE

Part I

Being - Self awareness

1. Place of birth/origin and acknowledgement of the deterrence/problem being faced aka statement of being and problem statement

2. Acknowledging the requirement for mitigation of problem being faced, say virtue, value or companionship

3. Allowing help/acceptance of or change in closed mindset to one of openness for all

Part II

Belonging - Social communication/self expression

4. Allowing release and acceptance of states of being at all times

5. Making peace with the presence

6. Acceptance of self

Part III, A

Communicating - Social communication etiquettes

7. Self expression

8. Sacrosanct code of conduct for public dialogues of self expression

9. Allowing mapping of self awareness to self and society

10. Being honest/truthful and building a growth mindset

Part III, B

Communicating- Acceptance/social awareness of self

11. Accepting oneness as the ultimate peace markup

12. Being aware in one's own capability and approaching the collaborative method by lack of comparison but by awareness of each other's strengths

13. See the pointlessness of hate, be humble and allow growth by equanimity, for one and all

14. Sustain inner peace by mindful and equitable understanding

15. Allow time for people to process the gap in communication/ patience

16. Choosing peace by being intuitive

17. The value of shared knowledge for levelling up one's own social awareness quotient

18. Practising collaborative communication

Part IV

Simplicity - Identification of belief systems, cohabitation and sustenance

19. Problem statement reassessment on a recurrent/regular/ need basis

20. Delimitation of problem with actualised/established norms

21. Create a collaborative approach towards self and society for thorough understanding

Part V

Authenticity - Revitalise authenticity, assertion and resolution

34

NARRATIVE

Part I
Being - Self awareness

Chapter 1. Place of birth/origin and acknowledgement of the deterrence/problem being faced aka statement of being and problem statement

Chapter 2. Acknowledging the requirement for mitigation of problem being faced, say virtue, value or companionship

Chapter 3. Allowing help/acceptance of or change in closed mindset to one of openness for all

CHAPTER 1

Place of birth/origin and acknowledgement of the deterrence/problem being faced aka statement of being and problem statement

What's in the name? Basically, gender, place of birth, lineage, emotions of what was the person perceived to be at birth and undeniably, an identity, that is fixed to the person.

Human beings are much like any social animal but our cognitive ability, however superior to any other species, controls our social functionality beyond one's cognitive perception.

You may be a natural vocalist but place of birth and identity perception during the early growth years, may have you believe an identity very different to your natural cognitive existence.

As is for most humans, once we are out of our chaperoned setting, we are free to acknowledge our natural selves by pathfinding for our own selves. That is when most adults come to terms with their natural abilities outside of the schooling and conditioning of the family and society.

Where's the problem in the manner, one may ask? It's in the discord between the identity we are made to believe, the actual human being we find ourselves to be, as we grow in years and experience and finding the right approach to communicating one's self to the society in a mutually beneficial manner. The discord one faces within oneself and in connecting with the society.

The quintessential existential quest of answers to 'being' aka the human consciousness, as observed, I am a being with an identity. The being is real and so is the identity. The being is the organic thinking feeling person and the identity is the social construct we have been made to believe and live.

Each is real because as much as I am in body and emotions, the same is affected by mental conditioning of the society. To differentiate one from the other is only possible in theory while the complex being lives in its ethereal complexity, striving everyday to be a better human being than before.

As independent individuals, we set our own standards. Standards unique to each person.

The goal is sustenance, an existence that is revitalised, each day anew.

We can begin where we are, because self awareness is not a linear process. There are no rules to reach and understand the self. We can start with an understanding of the intuitive self or we can start with our material existence/state of being. Either way, the realisation is absolute.

Curiosity to know one's true nature and being consciously aware is where it begins. One may call it enlightenment but it's a growth process every person actualises in life. A conscious awareness of our reasons for actions, motivations for the mind and that of the energy/spirit states of being.

It's only when we start approaching a mindset that is self-governed is when we become truly independent and it could be a conscious choice or a life occurrence.

Either way, the choice becomes imperative for a productive social function that is inclusive on the individual's part.

The reason for an individual aspiring to approach diversity and inclusion models could be for self-help, social help or for work.

Each step begins with the self, understanding of the reasoning, biases and need for diversity or inclusivity or inclusivity in diversity.

CHAPTER 2

Acknowledging the requirement for mitigation of problems being faced, say virtue, value or companionship

A collaborative existence depends on mutual affability that roots from an understanding and empathy for fellow beings.

The desire to exist ethically with authenticity and to practise mindful freedom of speech is easier said than done. Bringing about empathy for oneself requires having empathy for oneself. It begins with an understanding of the authentic self and our cognitive behavioural norms that are akin to us by nature and those that become us by practice.

Companionship that sustains life and livelihood is the virtue and value in the need for inclusivity in one's social communication. Empathy being the virtue and value that one seeks to practise in their social outlook.

Becoming/being a compassionate person in mind, body, soul is an internal journey, one that each person chooses to take upon in their own time of becoming, while social adherence begins at birth.

Hence, to perceive what is the best way of practising mindful freedom of speech, on public/social media/in society - a parity in perspective, which means a common ground needs to be arrived at, in one's own understanding of the self and the society.

Hearsay, a ground level unionisation of standards is essential for everyone to understand the context of any content/thought process.

This book is aligned to cater to a person's individualistic state of mind ahead of social understanding. Wherein, this chapter is pertaining to a person's intrinsic requirement as compared to social requirements.

Acknowledging one's own psychological make-up, even on a superficial level is enough to understand how to make peace with oneself. It's a simple one-step process, to be mindful.

Being intuitively mindful comes naturally to each one of us, however life situations and environment in consideration, comprehension is the first step to coherence and cohabitation.

It just takes some practice to identify, state and accept oneself, an art that takes some natural inherent ability and some training to be consistent.

Take up any plant found in almost every house in your locality.

Observe, these taken for granted beautiful specimens are a source of day-to-day joy. If only one practices being in the present moment often enough, a state of empathy emerges for nature and for oneself.

It's often that we take the most beautiful people or things for granted and it's only when we don't have it/them is when we realise the love and energy they bring to our lives.

Recognise something you have, that brings you a feeling of equity with the environment, in layman terms, anything that makes you feel normal and appreciate it.

It's in identifying one's own self, object, relative, society, situation or way of life in the routine that one sustains mindfulness everyday.

In sustainability for person, personnel or business context, the best working models function on the applied science between ethics/humanities and objective principle.

In order to connect the mindset to nature and humanities mindset such that intuitive mindfulness and sustenance becomes an ethical regular practice, as a beneficial and humane median, creating a sacrosanct code of conduct that retains the essence of one's own originality and is neutral in context is essential.

In-order to arrive at a stage where one can create comprehensive dialogues oneself, a dialogue within oneself is necessary.

Be it expressive or meditative is an individualistic decision.

Intuitiveness is unique as is everyone, it takes a moment to pause and listen to it.

CHAPTER 3

Allowing help/acceptance of or change in closed mindset to one of openness for all/ committing to self expression/vulnerability for growth

Compassion as strength is not the most novel concept. Kindness is the best virtue is a quotation, known to people, since time immemorial.

What's worth being memorial is the practice and proof of a life lived well as a compassionate existence, being practised dully. It takes courage to open our own mind to ourselves and believe in oneself/to be able to acknowledge ourselves truly to all.

A lot of people do not feel comfortable projecting their true belief systems to the world for fear of discomfort or miss-alignment with those who believe or live differently. While this discomfort may be genuine, what is given to oneself is the choice of self acceptance and development of a kind and compassionate state of mind that is inclusive for oneself and for others.

Being vulnerable to the self, creates an atmosphere and mindful acceptance of one's own virtues of being, enabling one with a growth mindset.

Contemplation of what was, what is, and what it's going to be -

The only productive thought that can arise from contemplating what was, is an understanding of self.

We know what it is, the present.

Happiness is a constant strife, it is never a concrete reality. We receive it in bits and pieces. When we have it, we say it would have been better if received in some other holistic fashion. When we are in want of it, we idolise a past or aspirational situation.

Time is in a continuous momentum, and in the existing scenario the previous one will be missed or a prospective one desired. It is a never ending cycle.

Some of us live in the world of what could be, a utopian existence. It bestows the traveller a beautiful, unfettered life.

There is no scope for anybody else to know our visualisations, be it of past glory, present mindfulness, future aspirations or utopian undertakings, unless we decide to share.

A choice to share, one step at a time, starting with this moment, this moment that is unique and precious is living in this moment.

In accepting the present moment, we identify nothing can be bracketed as independent. It's all correlated work in progress, the past, the present and the future.

'Be', by being the existence, the change, the acceptance that we seek in ourselves and society, we become an intrinsic and inclusive body/agent of inclusivity in diversity.

Part II

Belonging - Social communication/self expression

Chapter 4. Allowing release and acceptance of states of being at all times

Chapter 5. Making peace with the presence

Chapter 6. Acceptance of self

Chapter 4

Allowing release and acceptance of states of being at all times

Belong to the self, to belong to the community.

Charity begins at home, be it the mindset or the physical being.

The task here is not just to accept oneself for who we are but to acknowledge attributes that are constant and to consciously release variable attributes. By release of variables and acceptance of constants, finding the unidirectional truth of nowness.

As our days pass by, in the quest for something meaningful in life, or meaning of life, we seek meaning in forms of personal fulfilment, passion for work or spiritual alignment that quenches the heart and mind. Here, what we actually seek is a passion in life that shall keep one nourished and motivated at all times.

Like the reverence we have for people we idolise, we seek to be them in some way or the other, each person has an experienced, deemed, aspirational or personal idolised way of life. Something that to them seems to be the fixer of their own shortcomings or the correct way of becoming the aspirational being. What we need to realise is that it's our own wish and perspective to be something that we relate with in ourselves and have thus actualised it in a measure.

The acceptance of being the one who observes and wishes, brings about the wish in the inception of the thought. One has to acknowledge that it is always about one's own mindset and aspirational perspective. You are and it's your mind's journey of accepting gender, equality, life stage in a neutral/affirmative perceptiveness.

First step to belonging anywhere is to belong to oneself and then be open to learning and development.

CHAPTER 5

Making peace with the presence

Irrespective of place of birth and identity, life gives people their fair share of tough situations. To retain peace of mind in a diverse environment or an environment different from one's familiar perception, such that our own and another's inclusiveness is kept intact is work. Work that demands both intrinsic and extrinsic observation and adaptation by way of genuine evolution - the guide to being functional with integrity in any situation.

People generally appreciate strong, determined people. This trait might not be appreciated in a position that demands submissiveness.

Determination can stay to be a positive trait, even in an unfavourable situation.

The formula to crack this situational code is to take intuitive ethical action at all times, sustaining sanity and purpose in both situations of familiar and foreign interface.

When one does not understand the environment, the correct route is the intuitive and pragmatic way and then, when we have actualised the truth of the situation, the goodness and forward stance is sustained by staying on the good path.

People go through transitory phases throughout life. The transformation is different and unique for each person. People are generally expected and allowed to find their career and life path according to socially deemed benchmarks and then they are expected to reform to generic social ways of consistency, eg. marriage and stable career aspirations.

Throughout transitory or even stable situations wherein a coherent communication is required for equity and parity, a strong-willed approach, can enable a transition that sustains values and virtues constant to a person while they might not be aligned with the generic group they wish to comprise.

The only way to approach resolution in either way is acceptance and openness for oneself. One must belong to themselves before they wish to belong in a group.

That's the only way one can exist in a co-functional environment allowing respect and space for everyone.

We deal with any situational difficulty by coping with it and being through it and it's the mind that has to find new ways of coping with the situation to get better.

The objective is to make peace in nothingness by letting go of personal biases for the self, basically building self confidence by truth, to reach a stable and healthy mind and body.

Meeting mental well-being goals, driving confidence in having matured through it all and going back to the aspirational environment, as a more understanding human being.

The routes are different for everyone, to everyone who's been there and is still keeping ground.

Let's make it work.

CHAPTER 6

Acceptance of self

The state of belonging or being absolutely confident in one's own existence, be it factual and material or of the mind and self perceptiveness, is a constant.

States of being and that of mind are deemed to be in a constant momentum throughout life, for evolution, but the fact about acceptance of the authentic self is that it's an irreversible phenomenon.

Once you are aware of the constants of your own existence that make up the elementary and core composition of your being, you have arrived at a stage of being and acceptance of the unique entity that is yourself in the overall system of existence. It is neither deterred nor does it deter because peace of constance is a natural element to the natural state of being.

To enable these states of acceptance and tranquillity, we take time, work, and observation of the self.

To be in the moment, be intuitive and present and calm. Meditate then mediate.

Belonging to oneself is the toughest to realise and the easiest all the same. Ever tried understanding somebody who really admires you, how they see you and what it is that they admire in you? When we do so, we may or may not realise the other person's reason but we sure do find ourselves.

Being kind to one's own self has everything to do with acceptance and evolution by self observation. It's a understanding that we are human and we learn and falter or falter and learn and conscience is what keeps us on track and there's always scope for improvement, also, there has always been good in the self to come to the point of this internal revelation.

56

Part III, A

Communicating - Social communication etiquettes

Chapter 7. Self expression

Chapter 8. Sacrosanct code of conduct for public dialogues of self expression

Chapter 9. Allowing mapping of self awareness to self and society

Chapter 10. Being honest/truthful and building a growth mindset

58

CHAPTER 7

Self expression

Rules for self expression pertaining to diversity and inclusion,

1. Tone of communication.

2. Point of view.

3. Patience for time lag in social gaps.

Believe in oneself, everyone has their own timing and speed.

Believe in yourself for real and express yourself genuinely.

To do so, observe oneself, intuitively communicate, and have patience.

Looking at the context in a universal semblance for an inclusive mindset.

The finite and infinite form of being or life is energy. It's not a multidimensional infinity circle as contemporary design thinking would make us believe, scientifically, it's just quantum by quantum placement of photons, enabled into atoms, at a higher form as matter and emerge as photons again on disambiguation.

Similarly, we are everything we wish to be and everything we know us to be.

Tone of communication

An understanding, first of the mind and the body, then of that of the nature of spirit or life energy integrated and synthesised, enables us to see that human existence is one of harmonised mind/body/spirit complex.

This realisation of the state of being, i.e, human existence is a harmonised mind/body/spirit state/complex is the cognitive ability to perceive oneness of mind, body and the self-sustaining life energy.

Actualization, of the self and then of the existential or social order is the first step to attaining a third person/high level or overarching view of the situation.

Attainment of an actualized perception for inclusiveness in diversity, an actualized, three/multi-dimensional outlook is the first step to maintaining a neutral tone in one's social communication.

Thus, nurturing the self by meditative warmth and well being and sharing it with others.

Point of view

Singular/first person, second person or third person approach as per cognitive perception of requirement.

The divine energy, called 'Shiva' in Hinduism and 'stillness in movement' in Taoism, is a semblance of movement of vital energy and positivity within each individual. Understandably, the self-sustaining vital life energy within oneself.

The divine energy of 'Hari' in Hinduism or the Budhha's way in Buddhism, is a reference to the pathway of life of well-being, called the 'unconditional love' that is the 'truth about life'.

Understanding of the two pathways of the same energy, within and outside of singular human capacity leads to the understanding of infinite intelligence aka cognizance aka self and social awareness.

An understanding of the unitive significance of life and beings, gives one an empathy and cognizance for one and the other.

When addressing people for inclusivity, the communication must pertain to the order of person as required.

Narrative example, 'I am worthy of peace, fun, joy, freedom, harmony and beauty.' and 'Your efforts matter and you do too.', usage of singular first and second person approach respectively, in narration, when addressing one person.

'We, ourselves, can set ourselves free.', this is an example of inclusive approach to third person/group or collective narration.

Patience for time lag in social gaps

Practising scientific mindfulness in social communication.

The power to moderate one's own mind can only be realised by oneself.

Narrating the scientific mind and matter context in divinity, ideological semblance of cognizance or self and social awareness by the representation of 'Shiva' and 'Hari' in Hinduism.

Attaining 'Shiva' means internal actualization of the self. In nature, the feminine energy creates and nourishes and the male energy protects and sustains.

The energy form of 'Shiva' denotes an actualized form of both energies, one that is capable of creation, sustenance and protection. Ideologically a peaceful rejuvenation of the self-sustaining being, complete in oneself.

Similarly, mindfulness celebrated in the form of representation of 'Hari' is the healthy mindful way of interacting with the external environment and creating, nurturing, sustaining and protecting well-being.

Both ideological semblances, practised and mastered, give one, a scientifically mindful existence. Awarding one with self and social awareness, and peace of mind, actualised by way of semantic, logical coherence of the intangible elements of humane society.

Practising patience and mindfulness for self and allowing time for one to correctly gauge the gap in social communication, is embedded in one's practice of self-sustaining a calm state of being.

Creating, nurturing, sustaining a calm state of mind enables one to sustain, nurture, create or protect a society, i.e, an absolute existence of well-being, diverse and inclusive.

CHAPTER 8

Sacrosanct code of conduct for public dialogues of self expression

Why would one need to express oneself in society? Community functions on connection. We identify, connect and co-exist. The rule for communal living is kindness.

That said, what's the best route to connection at social setups like work and for essential collaborations? As practised diligently and found true, it has to root from within, from oneself. Kindness for oneself and others practised diligently is the answer.

'Cogito ergo sum', translated into 'I think therefore I am' is a universal age old philosophy by Rene Descrates. It's a form of self and social validation of being.

Ascertaining, that the presence of 'thought' mandates and validates the existence of the thinker.

Arriving at a peaceful place of mind and heart requires dialogue and it might not always be the most eloquent essay with mannerisms at par with required standards. Here's my personal rant.

Author's note - 'You think therefore you are. It is proof enough of one's being but the proof of your intelligence is not in the mere fact that you think, the proof of your intelligence is in the substance of your thought.

If thought is the basis on which we acknowledge the existence of the being, do acknowledge the existence of a being in animals as well.

Descartes did not make any statement pertaining to animals but as is observed, animals are sentient beings and exhibit thought for their own self and the wellbeing of other sentient beings.

It is not just the ability to think and deduct that makes human kind an intellectually higher being, it is our will power.

The will power to decide how to think, to look for good in people and situations, to know when to act and when to stop.

I have come to a place where I see how amazing a species we are and how blind of our own worth. We are blind to all that is good in us, to the rare ability of having a will, to be better, to think for a greater good, but we are quite aware of a smart, thinking, analytical mind.

We gloat about being able to construe, see logic and have analytical thinking, but how do we use it?

To pass judgments left, right and centre.

Judgments based on how we see the world, oblivious to the fact that there is never a single reality. Oblivious to the fact that we will never know the entirety of a situation.

The human mind is not designed to know everything, it is limited as long as we are limited in our outlook towards the world, towards life.

Such debates take the usual course and I find myself surrounded by a majority that doesn't even care as to where we are headed, nothing appeals to them except their own woes and wants; and then, there is this minority which understands but glorifies in its ability to see beyond the usual and does nothing about it.

The worst are the pseudo intellectuals, the ones who find themselves the most intelligent, the ones who think they understand everything, everybody, every situation. The ones who know there are no boxes but they will still put others in them, white box, black box, grey box. The ones who think they can fit in by way of understanding.

Why can't somebody be something we do not understand?

My heart tells me I am abstract and so is everything else, always subject to change, ever evolving.

Heart takes the lead, the mind thinks too much.'

This blog that I wrote in 2017, over the course of time, enabled me to understand the constants and variables of my being. Grit, authenticity and grace being constant to my being and the situational perception to be the variable. Being abstract, metaphysical, is the true nature of the mind but there are characteristic attributes of the being that are constant to each one of us.

The sacrosanct code of conduct is to be of kind and considerate composition at all times, by being honest to oneself, rant to oneself maybe, and then see, we ourselves are being limited in our assessment of the capacity for everyone to evolve into better and in the momentous nature of time.

CHAPTER 9

Allowing mapping of self awareness to self and society by being honest/truthful

Self awareness is an understanding, both cognitive and intuitive, of the ways in which we are conditioned to think and behave and the ways in which nature gifted us in being. This mapping of two mutually independent but connected traits when brought together in an individual, is the basis of understanding and coming to terms with one's self. This is also a mirror effect when we willfully allow this mapped sense to commune in society.

Society is a mirror reflection of us in ways. The social conditioning, be it temporary or staunch, that is characteristic of one's nativity, is perceived in the identity of an individual.

A person may believe in the mirror that society reflects on them/him/her or may identify with their social image, or may not be able to believe in the social construct of themselves that is given to them.

Coherence or mapping one's own comfort in identity with one comprehensible by everyone, society, is bestowed to some, some make it happen. The authenticity and truth in self identification is the core guiding principle for self enabled mindfulness and hence peace of mind that sustains. The sustained calm in one's reflective sense that has been found true to the fabric of the mind and individual composition, this is the essence that sustains one's being when mapped with society.

Primal instincts nourished, nurtured, sophisticated for honest communication is one's own doable action. 'Karma path' is the performing action without attachment to the outcome because it emerges from and for the sake of truth and well-being of all. The doable action is to stay on the path of consciousness and conscious living and to take it beyond oneself in kindness and action.

Success for people is of mind, body, soul, well-being and/or all of it.

One's dharma is to stay on the path of consciousness and conscious living and to take it beyond.

When people desire emotional valuation or acquisition, they tend to appease and attract.

In case of material validation or acquisition, a material projection is demonstrated. While, in the case of spiritual fulfilment, one has to align their material and emotional being with a rightful intent.

To achieve a sense of self awareness that is mapped to one's own ratio of success, one has to focus on the present, actual self and state of being.

Being grounded makes one aware.

That's what is needed to have three dimensional perceptiveness for mapping the self to society.

To achieve this, focus on whatever it is. Sustainable social communication requires shifting and expansion from a perspective of oneself to one of inclusivity. Eventually encompassing three points of view, one's own, another's and that of the community as a collective.

The highest/most peaceful or sustainable level of agreement is when I or the system is self-aligned, aligned with the singular other and the point of view is agreeable and aligned with/beneficial to the community or society.

The first level of work to be done is being aligned, finding the core components or essence of being. Then, by communicating, relating and resonating with others, we build connected communities that believe in a common goal.

Self sufficiency, consistent connectivity, publicly acknowledged value and valuation is what one needs to have arrived at a point of individual sufficiency.

Pragmatic assessment of social reality and internal biases is the core requirement to reach, connect and to stay true to the common goal of wellbeing via communication.

To be consistent in the pursuit of self, originality and social outcomes, to begin with, one has to acknowledge the primary nature, the original mindful existence. What a person does consistently in life with diligence becomes their default mindset to connect and perceive the society and the self.

Contentment and abundance when practised as a mindset leads to realising the evolved social nature. The highest form of existential being is aligned with spirit science, the life energy we derive and consume by our existential choices.

All three components of mind, diligence and life energy, postulated and aligned, gives one the success mantra for social communication.

This statement is substantiated with Aristotle's theory that argumentative appeals are of three types, logical, ethical, and emotional/ logos, ethos, pathos.

Thus an efficient mechanism of social communication that adheres to inclusion in diversity for all includes the three rational elements of being and focuses on one's actual existence.

Categorically,

A. Mindful awareness and creation

B. Rightful intent and considerate action

C. Purposeful action based on virtues

D. Focus on intuitive clarity

Thoroughly aligned/mapped components, thus communicated as messages for parity, bring about well-being and progress for the entity as a whole.

CHAPTER 10

Having a growth mindset

Patience within is not just for others but for oneself. Patience to be at peace with all that has been and is, sustaining a calm with everything that has been done and taking a moment to accept it without bias as an honest part of one's journey, opens one to new perspectives of existence.

The moment taken to process what is and what could be is the existential occurrence of nothingness. Vitality of this space, takes one to that which occupies the space, the vacant stillness that makes way for moving ahead with a positive mindset. It's a recurrent choice to intuitively accept the self and inculcate the mindset.

This chapter of The D&I Manual aka the diversity and inclusion construct, a step by step actualisation of the implementation model is the bridge between the self and the society, the final narrative and approach towards self acceptance.

One needs to finally rise above oneself and be peaceful, then mindfully and constructively, be beneficially inclusive of the other and then the environment.

Actualising strength and the impact of communications when we wish to align our core values with the society we comprise.

Author's note - My core values are ethics, originality, dexterity and compassion. There's a story I heard as a kid, of a man who was to be considered truly strong if he could withstand the cold weather by standing in the river all night long. He did. When the king asked him how he could do it, he answered that the glow from the lighthouse gave him strength. He was declared not to be truly there for having sought motivation outside.

A paper, I read, about 'giving and giving in', states that researchers found that often the act of giving is inspired by the gratification and hence labelled as impure altruism.

I contemplate, this is quite like the duality of impact in ethical business. The propagation of corporate social responsibility and the beneficial aspects that organisations generally seek out, are considered ethically mutually disparate, however materially aspirationally conjoined.

Same goes for being, when we do good, we do good for the sake of good. When we create inclusivity by being good, for ourselves and by being inclusive of others, it has to be genuine for the self and the other to perceive, gauge and trust the process.

Being truly self inspired/ethical needs awareness, embodiment and results as proof.

In life, often the giving action is inspired by intuition of doing something right even when the reasons are not clear at that point of time. That's the guiding principle we seek, gratification is a by-product that is realised much later and without having sought it.

For ethical social efficacy and to gauge social efficiency of one's action, intuition is the guiding principle during the process and gratification the stepping stone to knowing the path was right.

Since, success is deemed to be a combination of self inspired, actualized and proven-in-reality, action. The situational analysis for the desired outcome of social success is self sufficiency, implementation, profitability, aligned with ethics.

Communication has a major impact in aligning values at work.

Let's say, in the story, the man had stood in the river knowing anything might happen and had still done the right thing relying on nothing but pure grit, then he would have been considered absolutely self inspired, morally righteous and strong.

As the story goes he was considered not to be strong enough - is it right for the governing body to assess him this critically or was it a lag in communication on the protagonist's part?

What if he had tried with pure grit and failed?

In my perspective, the situation needed appropriate communication and sustenance of calm from all parties involved in the situation/event. Since, life is always work in progress, self confidence and social vindication both situations are subjective.

The fact is, there is always scope to outdo ourselves and be stronger intrinsically and externally and this measure requires sustenance and a favourable approach.

In the story, the man was declared failed by the king. When I heard this story, I felt the pathos, the over critical assessment and the fatality of consideration, the only thing I could think of - I am sure there's something more that can be done.

When we are not right there, we seek motivation/gratification until we reach there.

When we are right there, we look for what more can be done, externally and intrinsically for betterment for a pro-growth mindset.

Mindfulness serves as the bridge/connection.

Parity by empathy for self and others is the final step to have come up with a mindset that is appropriate for social communication for inclusivity.

Part III , B

Communicating- Acceptance/social awareness of self

CHAPTER 11

Accepting oneness as the ultimate peace markup.

Accepting oneness as the ultimate social markup for the sustenance of calm and collaborative states of mind.

As the first three parts of the book take one through specific mind maps of being, belonging and communicating ethically, this part sustains the constancy/practice/exercise of the first three parts of the book and ascertains an individual's perceptions of self and comprehensive existence in the society, for oneself.

One may perceive this to be looking at oneself from a social perspective but in adherence it still has to be practised in essence from one's own vantage point. This retains the constants of one's being, which have already been actualized and also gives a realistic view of one's self in society, the basic requirement for considering oneself as part of the whole/the society. Seeing oneself in oneness with the collective whole that we call community.

Hence, the ultimate markup for peace and mindfulness in one's approach towards accepting oneness in society, also called being inclusive and diverse in mindset.

Learning by doing, self acceptance is a conscious and deliberate statement of the factual being and aspects pertaining to the atmosphere that need stating, hence accepting oneness as the ultimate peace markup.

Acknowledging self with the community is realising, one is community.

A shift in perspective from individualistic self to social self, enables functional and ethical social communication that is inclusive at all times.

Author's note - 'An average mid-income upbringing means that you come from an upper middle-class family, your parents sent you to the best schools in your city and you were expected to qualify for the best possible state/national/global universities for yourself. This group generally does not have the privilege of thinking too far off though, like a career in music or the movies. However, extracurricular hobbies are highly cherished as side gigs, for fun.

Gender is, generally, neutral and we grow up fairly equally. Moral values and virtues are equal for boys and girls.

Those who are lucky and get to work in that same deemed class, live happily.

However, if anyone ever gets brave, moves out of nativity, or leaves perfectly well-paying jobs, they'll have known a different narrative.

I had this idea about equality, and it has evolved over time.

As I travelled and interacted with more people, the idea of equitable access took form and while there's so much more to be understood in the quest for life and work-life balance, there's one thing that's become quite apparent to me. Life and I mean the primordial life energy, is persistent and perpetual. It evolves, takes new forms and lives on.

It's up to us to make peace with it and find joy in all phases of it.'

This book aims to bring parity in one's own perspective and thus in our approach towards society and others.

Mindfulness is the best route to inculcate a healthy mindset consistently.

CHAPTER 12

Being aware in one's own capability and approaching the collaborative method by lack of comparison but by awareness of each other's strengths

Equity in strength for D&I, is by way of mutual respect of unique strengths attune to each individual in a community.

Lack of comparison and being impartial in one's external perspective/outlook is achieved by continuous and sustained peace of mind, attained by meditation and self actualisation which results in mindfulness

To be considerate and aware of another's perspective and hence strengths is easy to perceive equivocally when we become impartial and patient. Patience and mutual understanding governs growth while in actualization, to grow through what we go through.

For inclusivity or peaceful thought perception, the influence or social worth of social communication is dependent and assessed on usability, wellbeing, freedom of speech and emotional, mental health, all of it liable to good self governance and individual mindset.

To strive for balance through or by enabling inclusivity requires effective outreach. Equity requires a mutual perceptiveness of strength and lags. This is the pathway for effective mapping of mindsets to mediate the process of inclusivity. The task is to identify the point of adherence/parity and similarity, environment and the cultural setting and mapping the self and one's own values with the level of adherence that is possible within the social setup.

The Curious Case of Benjamin Button is a good movie that beautifully conveys the laws of connectivity and being - a baby born old, starts getting younger with time, lives a life in reverse order and dies by growing young enough to not exist.

An interesting movie to watch with many very famous quotations like 'opportunities are important, even those that we don't get.' The movie shows how everything is interconnected but the message at the end of the movie is my favourite -

"Some people were born to sit by a river, some to be struck by lightenin', some have an ear for music, some are artists, some know buttons, some know Shakespeare, some are mothers and some people can dance."

An authentic and conscious life rooted in one's own merits is sustainable and unique for each one of us.

The realisation of unique characteristics in one and all, objectively leads to sustainable/conscious life, which brings about balance in mind, body, soul, and society.

Even when people act out of personal motives and act righteously which converts into goodwill, this is still a conscientious and sustained sense of inclusivity for well-being.

CHAPTER 13

The pointlessness of hate, be humble and allow growth by equanimity, for one and all

Actual growth is in calm and communication that is substantial.

One may argue that noise and emotional venting for self expression is a way of authenticity.

Provenly, emotional venting, when found factually correct and understood coherently - it's only then can it be the correct pathway for solution to problems.

Emotional venting, say communication that is out of momentary/situational perception, and also humility in the face of adversity, are two coins of the same situation. Both given to extra or less vibrational depiction of one's situation, hence situationally felt but failing to be consistent for resolution.

Self-expression that is not just factual but that which conveys the gravity of the occurrence from a higher scale of perception are more attune to sensible perception by unaffected parties.

The pointlessness of hate is in the extraneous sentiment and humility is a virtue in all situations but the expression of the gravity of a situation has to be factual.

Levelling up one's sentiment to one of mindfulness, brings versatility and adaptability in one's social communication. Enabling new ways of thought expression.

Hence, valuation of the soft skills for growth and for inclusivity.

Effective and efficient communication is the bridge between the familiar and unfamiliar and from being biassed to neutrality.

The highly affable and highly unpleasant can be brought to a point of consensus with humility as the bridge and connecting link for affability and kind-consideration.

"Only the development of compassion and understanding for others can bring us the tranquillity and happiness we all seek." - Dalai Lama.

Humility makes one realise the unique talents of each individual and hence the best route to unity in diversity. When we believe in equality, we believe in the natural occurrence of one as a unique element and entity in the whole.

"When you find that anything agrees with reason and is conducive to the good and benefit of one and all, accept it and live up to it." ~ Buddha

"Compassion brings strength to our minds by lessening fear and increasing confidence. Doubts and irrational thinking decline. As a result, in the company of others the mind is relaxed, there are feelings of closeness, and we have a feeling that life has meaning and purpose." - Dalai Lama.

Authors note- As experienced, at a technology company product means software and portfolio means client data.

At knowledge centres, product and services means stakeholder deliverables, whatever it be, tech, comms, ops, finance support and portfolio means stakeholder relationship.

At a bank, product means investment products and portfolio means particular aspects of the investment product.

At fund houses, product means the investment type, eg. debt or equity and portfolio means the invested companies.

As seen, the same terminology has different meanings for each sector.

While it's fun to adapt to new ways of thinking and working, people often feel that their cerebral acumen is being taken for granted.

Hence, equality in cognitive ability should also be a D&I objective.

The self approach to achieving equity in mind and matter require comprehension, statement and validation of

1. Human self/to oneself/one's own capabilities

2. Social self/to oneself and others/social mapping of self

3. Values as a whole/in third person/social mapping of one's own values with the community

The eventual, three dynamic understanding is the result of this pathway, leading to peace and mitigation of negativity, hate, comparison.

CHAPTER 14

Sustain inner peace by mindful and equitable understanding

The affectionate sense of familiarity, love and belonging connects fraternities of any order.

Retention of one's own virtues of being, be it one of kindness or practised, conscious living, positions one on strong ethical ground.

The practice of conscious living merges the difference in our virtues to that of consciousness, both pathways being pro-growth and ethical for one and all.

While the sense of belongingness and parity connects individuals as a community, there are times when we choose to look at the differences within the community rather than the common ground.

Rejuvenation of one's own value system makes us stronger and gives us freedom. Money/strength/power dynamics are tangible elements, a value system rooted in core self belief that connects one to the community as a whole is evermore fulfilling on a humane level. Goal, propose, higher calling on humanitarian grounds are met when a person aligns one's core values to that of the community.

Community first values make apparent that one person's loss is not another person's gain, material values are time bound entities and value systems are constants depicting a person's character during tough situations that people remember and live by.

Building each other, building each and the other, hence building sustainable life for all.

CHAPTER 15

Allow time for people to process the gap in communication/ patience

Time spells everything as is, we have in our power to speak the truth but time-allocation for it to be processed and accepted by people to be gauged for exactly what was conveyed is not in our power. Neither does that mean that we do not speak our truth, nor that we live by aeons of timelines governed by others.

Do the right thing, do good unto yourself, for the tide of time to be forever yours.

Patience intune with time is the best measure for us to stay ethical which brings result-orientedness in a material or even in an ethereal world.

We have very little control over anything except ourselves. Allowing time for people to process the gap in communication takes diligence, action and patience and a ton of hope and good will.

Navigating through seasons of life, big and small things will come and go, some may stay too.

It's not about the big or the small things, it's about being intuitive in a diverse atmosphere, by way of logical acumen and the retention of a calm state of mind.

Time is a precious commodity and one must be inspired to spend life energy purposefully.

Train your mind to follow a routine or a schedule for retaining healthy habits.

Stay factual in mind, disconnect with anything that deludes the mind.

Connect with the community for real to create healthy social communication.

Take out time for oneself regularly and meditate for self alignment.

Meditate and sustain that which enables you to start with a fresh leap of energy.

CHAPTER 16

Choosing peace by being intuitive

Conscious living and leadership is a thought that has acquired value as people realise its actual essence is well-being.

The collaborative sentiment of staying true to goodness as strength in any situation of social state of being.

In adversity, conscious living garners more inner strength to stay positive, which is the original purpose of conscious living/ the thought concept as a way of life.

When one stays on the chosen path of positive action and right intent, this action brings about the social outcome of the society living consciously and collaborating for impactful growth.

Intention and intuitiveness being measures of intangible nature, tangibly gauging one's course by kindred adherence in a social environment and for inclusivity of self and others is achievable by practical action.

When practising soft skills for good, always keep others before yourself in mind and for beneficial attainment.

Stay true to one's virtues and intuitive ethical rules of existence, intuitive goodness to keep one on the path.

Since external behaviour can only be seen in action and not for intuition and intention, practice self governance at all times.

People judge one's own action by intent while other person's actions by their visible, tangible action.

Tangible action is the only way the overarching purpose driven social action can be assessed.

Thus inclusivity through structure has to be incorporated through conscious intuitive action first, by one and all.

The task here is to be the overarching purpose driven society, by a third person perspective approach and evolve one's social existence to that of a person mindful enough to be constructive and calm at all times.

CHAPTER 17

The value of shared knowledge for levelling up one's own social awareness quotient

Knowledge, given or taken, which is shared acumen, is basically the functional fabric of society and community living.

The positive momentum of learning better by sharing motivates people to share selflessly, for the betterment of the human race. Humans as social beings not only rejoice in companionship, but also grow by mutual connection, be it intuitive action or factual collaboration.

Growth is not only of material goods but also of goodness. A growth mindset that creates a more beneficial and nurturing atmosphere becomes possible by fine tuning one's cognitive function of social awareness. Self-enabled social awareness is a result of mastering constant attributes of one's being and then mastering the constants of the environment that we belong/originate from as an individual and a group.

The value of shared knowledge for levelling up one's own social awareness quotient depends on the understanding of the twofold nature of survival, for yourself and for others - an internal mirror for self perception and an external guideline for social communication and interaction.

Self perception is one's own measure of being and belonging, that is grace and kindness.

External guidelines for social communication and interaction are required to sustain goodness. Practising contentment consciously and channelizing it in oneself and others.

Author's note - A mandala of positivity, mindfulness, and gratitude helps me get to terms with my consciousness and being.

Born in a religious Hindu household, I have always acknowledged and seen the powerfully positive vibes prayers and spiritual rituals create. Even now when I hear the conch shell trumpet, it stirs all the goodness and godliness in me and I take it beyond.

Hailing from Allahabad from the maternal side, I have been to Prayagraj since I was a kid. Not only was I made to take a dip in the holy Ganges but was taken all the way to Sangam - the spot where the three holy rivers meet (Ganga, Yamuna, Saraswati). It's an old memory and I remember clearly seeing two different shades of water. I said so and was told that Saraswati had almost vanished. I thought of the Kalyug era being vacant of good knowledge. Ever since then I have observed and seen that the names given, contexts mentioned in the religious books and versions, have a very real, material and mindful implication in life.

It is not that we don't know good from bad, generally or logically to survive people tend to follow the ruling practice to survive. If Saraswati vanishes, to live, drink what's available.

However, if you feel unquenched by the impurity, cleanse the water available, make it pure. The three rivers come from the same source and acquire different minerals, textures based on the natural course, hence the unique character.

Contentment is as much about what we have, as much about creating and purifying what's required. When we can do so in mind and matter, we'll know the continuous and constant source of goodness in us as splendid as the mighty Himalayas and the sparklingly pure Ganges.

Be your own source of positivity and happiness, channelise it in others.

What a beautiful world it would be if we all lived for good.'

To do,

1. Sustain goodness.

2. Practice contentment consciously.

3. Channelize it in oneself and others.

CHAPTER 18

Practising collaborative communication

Aspects of dimensions of existence-

1. A mindset that is positive, mindful and gracious.

2. Action or karma that is determined and productive/ creative.

3. Consciousness and attention

Diagrammatically representation of the above said would look like functional aspects being conjoined by values of existence, creating a functional essence that is unique to each individual.

Directly aligning one's values with effective communication.

Author's note - The original ability to wonder is what is unique to each person.

Everyone is born to be something original to themselves, some are artists, some are mothers, some are dancers.

Finding one's originality and being it, makes one peaceful and content, which enables an overall kindred sense of being.

In my childhood days , we used to reach school way in advance for the morning assembly. It was just a bunch of us and the only source of refuge open was the assembly hall and the library.

That's where I found my love for new ideas in books and in the tranquillity of a library.

When I started working, at each of my jobs I was motivated to do more, learn more, like finding new books to explore.

Although the world's not a library, we need to learn to ask for whatever it is that we need, out loud and in the most pleasant and practical way possible.

Social communication has it protocols,

1, Grace - Gratitude for all that's good.

2. Community - Telling people they make the world a better place.

3. Reminders - Sharing thoughts and memoirs.

4. Opinions - Sharing points of view and understanding the world better from everyone's point of view.

5. Assistance- Being supportive in whatever capacity possible.

6. Fun- It's so much more fun connecting for more creativity.

The above behavioural aspects considered, analogy/representation for ideal social communication.

How one functions in society can be mapped by a question and answer format to understand one's own social equity.

Shared here is a Q&A sample created and supplied by the author. -

    A. I have always been a - stoic.

    B. How society functions - has always been a pensive case study to me, I have always had my own thoughts and opinions on everything.

C. When you say you need - anything, some people genuinely help, some judge.

D. How do people react - is specific to each one of them.

E. They identify - themselves with people and situations/relativity and think from their range of ease, proximity and comfort/resonance.

Deducing an ideal formula for social communication that is inclusive at all times. -

Studying management in media and comms, we were two sorts, vocal and nonchalant. The vocal ones wanted PR/Ad in mainstream media houses and the nonchalant ones loved corporate/business communication.

In the next few years, it all got mixed. Mainstream media one's got sober and got into corporations, corporate ones got more enthused and became more vocal and today, it looks like we are all somewhere in the middle. Everyone is balanced and vocal about what matters to them.

Since social communication is purpose driven, for well-being, sorting the communication into objective and subjective approaches gives it a sorted analogy.

Objective (joy, community, growth) and purposeful subjective (opinion to know better) interactions make one feel justified.

Identify for the self, make your own usability metric of communication and create sensible, decipherable, collaborative and purpose driven conversations.

Part IV

Simplicity - Identification of belief systems, cohabitation, sustenance

Chapter 19. Problem statement reassessment on a recurrent/regular/ need basis

Chapter 20. Delimitation of problems with actualised/established norms

Chapter 21. Create a collaborative approach towards self and society for thorough understanding

CHAPTER 19

Problem statement reassessment on a recurrent/regular/ need basis

Identification of belief systems and consistent mapping of the virtues for cohabitation and sustenance, is the three step pathway to regulating good practices and reassessing them recurrently.

Identification of belief systems is simplicity for action.

Do it, be the actionable verb. Stay calm at all times.

Mapping the same/cohabitation is mindfulness via acceptance of the oneness of self and everything else.

Enabling a growth mindset and finally building a mind and environment that is peaceful and accepting of oneself and the other is simply an act of identification of belief systems for cohabitation and sustenance.

A product summary of this book would be a pro-growth sustainability hack by way of self actualised inclusivity in diversity.

Similarly, what does an individual need to have achieved to be an agency of inclusivity, what do we need to sustain growth?

Problem statement reassessment on a recurrent/regular/ by way of,

1. Patience
2. Understanding
3. Practice

Cycle of life is directly linked to life cycle and it is dependent on state of mind/mindset.

A person who is whole on one's own is functional and of sound mindset and states of mind at all times.

CHAPTER 20

Delimitation of problems with actualised/established norms

Actualised and established norms for inclusive social communication,

- equity by way of awareness and acceptance.

Statement of facts, not just one's own but perception, understanding of facts for society, like labour laws and the fundamental rights of individuals as per constitution, that adhere to and emphasis on gender equity, equality, focus on zero differentiation and enable approbation, equate differences by way of awareness and acceptance of socially validated and accepted norms for equality.

Conventionality is fabricated but a lot of the laws have known the test of aeons and been found suitable. Knowledge of norms that stay the same across generations helps one practice self righteousness that is aligned not just with the contemporary but social laws found good for all.

Self righteousness when as per convention that is profound is consistent. Being conventionally moral has nothing to do with personal religious philosophy. Convention is social appropriation. Self righteousness is self appropriation. Both are subject to belief and when the belief is equality, a factual adherence is the answer.

Inclusivity must root out of scientific facts and sensible laws, it is only then that it is sustained and aligned.

An aligned sense of self and convection is completion of a person's individualistic approach to existence that is beneficial for one and all.

Shared here is an example of the fundamental rights as per the Constitution of India and the United Nations human rights mandates for the law of the land.

Each country mandates their own, a knowledge of the same and then referenced well, gives global laws of equality.

Fundamental Rights, Constitution of India - The Constitution offers all citizens, individually and collectively, some basic freedoms. These are guaranteed in the Constitution in the form of six broad categories of Fundamental Rights, which are justifiable. Article 12 to 35 contained in Part III of the Constitution deals with Fundamental Rights. These are:

Right to equality, including equality before law, prohibition of discrimination on grounds of religion, race, caste, sex or place of birth, and equality of opportunity in matters of employment.

Right to freedom of speech and expression, assembly, association or union, movement, residence, and right to practise any profession or occupation (some of these rights are subject to security of the State, friendly relations with foreign countries, public order, decency or morality).

Right against exploitation, prohibiting all forms of forced labour, child labour and traffic in human beings.

Right to freedom of conscience and free profession, practice, and propagation of religion.

Right of any section of citizens to conserve their culture, language or script, and right of minorities to establish and administer educational institutions of their choice; and Right to constitutional remedies for enforcement of Fundamental Rights.

The United Nations Declaration specifying 'basic human rights'-

The Preamble of the UN's Declaration specifies that the 'basic rights of humans' should be protected by the rule of law, and that all members of the human family are granted these equal and inalienable rights, which form the foundation of freedom, justice, and peace in the world. Much like the United States Declaration of Independence and similar documents throughout history, the Universal Declaration of Human Rights universally protects fundamental human rights and lays down the obligation of governments to act when rights are violated. Here is a list of basic human rights that are included within the UDHR: All human beings are born free and equal in dignity and rights. They are endowed with reason and conscience and should act towards one another in a spirit of brotherhood.

Everyone is entitled to all the rights and freedoms set forth in this Declaration, without distinction of any kind, such as race, colour, sex, language, religion, political or other opinion, national or social origin, property, birth or other status. Furthermore, no distinction shall be made on the basis of the political, jurisdictional or international status of the country or territory to which a person belongs, whether it be independent, trust, non-self-governing or under any other limitation of sovereignty.

Everyone has the right to life, liberty and security of a person.

No one shall be held in slavery or servitude; slavery and the slave trade shall be prohibited in all their forms.

No one shall be subjected to torture or to cruel, inhuman or degrading treatment or punishment.

Everyone has the right to recognition everywhere as a person before the law.

All are equal before the law and are entitled without any discrimination to equal protection of the law. All are entitled to equal protection against any discrimination in violation of this Declaration and against any incitement to such discrimination.

CHAPTER 21

Create a collaborative approach towards self and society thorough understanding

Three years back I wrote an article on LinkedIn, namely - '8th March 2020. It's a legacy.' that received some level of attention. Generally because the caption is interesting and while my article was inspired by corporate legacy systems, little did I fathom but soon did I realise that building legacy systems in family, organisations and person is the ultimate dream for many.

I wrote a basic article that conveyed the meaning and concluded on the note that I believe in women being out there and making it happen for themselves.

The reference to the article refers to my evolution.

My perspective on managing one's own life has changed or evolved since then. Women need to manage family and professional responsibilities in a very different light than their male peers. Some aspects are time bound and can be as per their choice, while others are per social norms. Hence, we prioritise and focus to equate and equip ourselves with the right mindset that strengthens our possibilities and enables us to achieve our full potential.

Evolution is a thing, also the basics of physical and psychological being, combined and understood well, a growth mindset becomes possible. The goodness in inculcating a growth mindset is in the achievement of an evolved state of understanding and being.

Part V

Authenticity - Revitalise authenticity, assertion and resolution

22. Process statement for overarching recognition of purpose

23. Vindication/validation of functionality by users

CHAPTER 22

Process statement for overarching recognition of purpose

Recognition of purpose is in being.

Experiences should be used for beneficial understanding of situations.

Begin now, with this very moment being a perception of newness, of self, another or society.

Pick something, anything, one thing, breathe in, accept it as your own.

You have created. Already. Repeat. In any way you feel great about it.

Revitalising authenticity for assertion and resolution -

Step 1. Create your own matric/mantra/mechanism by way of understanding the functionality of the self and that of the society.

Step 2. Belief in intuitive self is the way, through and through, all ways.

CHAPTER 23

Vindication/validation of functionality by users

Revitalization of value and virtues is validated and vindicated by way of assertion and is revived in its actual essence by resolution. The process of making a system self sustained and everlasting in essence.

The D&I Manual is a thesis that devises a model divided into five stages of cognitive learning, development and communication.

Each stage is depicted as part and narrative in this book. Actualising of each stage is unique to each individual and is also perpetual. Over a span of a person's life, every stage requires situational understanding and assessment of the fulfilment required.

A thorough understanding and practical adherence to the manual to the self, situational and social condition is the way to acquire peace within and around and a stoic stance in life that is perpetual and perpetuates good will.

There's one way to be functional. -

By doing.

It's in being.

It's in doing your thing.

It's in making it generic.

Be yourself, authentically and soulfully.

Be the self, there's one way to be oneself.

Being - in this moment of being lies acceptance of oneself, of another and an approach to acceptance and openness to more and diverse.

Being inclusive of oneself and another.

REFERENCE

- **CONSTITUTION OF INDIA**
- **THE UPANISHADS, EKNATH EASWARAN**
- **KARL MARX, CAPITAL, A CRITICAL ANALYSIS OF CAPITALIST PRODUCTION**
- **A SHORT HISTORY OF THE WORLD, H. G. WELLS**
- **METAPHYSICS, ARISTOTLE**
- **UNITED NATIONS PREAMBLE TO 'UNIVERSAL DECLARATION OF HUMAN RIGHTS'**
  www.un.org/en/about-us/universal-declaration-of-human-rights

116

ABOUT THE AUTHOR

Shipra Tripathi is a business communication professional with extensive, multidisciplinary, technical acumen across diverse sectors. She has worked in India in various technology, financial and commercial corporations.

She is a Master's in Business Administration in Communication Management, Class of 2014 from SIMC, Bangalore, Symbiosis International University, India and Bachelor of Pharmacy, Class of 2012, from Bundelkhand University, Jhansi, U.P., India.

'The D&I Manual' is her communications and corporate governance thought module, out of her work experience and study.

She objectively pursued an in-depth programme to gauge her expertise acquired in the Indian domain to global standards, Executive Education - Value Based Leadership Online Programme, Yale, School of Management, October - December 2021.

Her keen interest in humanities and theology is the primary guiding principle for this book.

EPIGRAPH

The author's passion for communication, both vocational and avocational gave form to 'The D&I Manual'

'Myriads of colour, scents, vibes, to be perceived in one sight.
Amongst all this I saw a light.
Bright, warm, carefree yet serene.
Shining not just for self but for all those whose light was getting dimmer.
The vibrations were entrancing, when it reached my soul, I was enlightened.
I realise that we all have our own light but sometimes an aid is necessary for it to ignite.'

The Light (2010)
Shipra Tripathi